I0468530

From a Stream To a River

Finding Success and Achieving Your Goals

By

Warren Philip Gates

Copyright © 2015 by Warren Philip Gates
All rights reserved. This book or any portion thereof may not be
reproduced or used in any manner whatsoever without the express
written permission of the publisher except for the use of brief
quotations.

Two Lessons from My Grandfather

On a hot summer day, the summer after my sixth grade graduation, my next door neighbor and I pulled a card table and two chairs out onto the front lawn, wrote lemonade on a giant poster board, made up a huge pitcher, and waited. And waited.

After some time, my grandfather came outside and asked us what we were doing. We told him all about our plans to buy baseball cards and lollipops at the end of the day. And then he asked us a question.

Who is paying you?

We looked around. No one was paying us at the moment, but we had high hopes. He then made a suggestion. He said we should take a walk through the neighborhood and ask everyone we saw if they would like a glass of lemonade. Once we knew better who would like lemonade on a hot summer day we would be able to make the right amount; we could even take the wagon and deliver lemonade to them.

We all want to be successful. When I was young I wanted my lemonade stand to provide me with all the baseball cards I could get my hands on, but since then my priorities have changed. I no longer want an enormous stack of baseball cards, but I still want to be successful.

Who is paying you?

Understanding who is paying you is one of the most important elements in wealth building. It may seem too simple, and you may want to skip over this part, but believe me, understanding who pays you can make all the difference.

It relates to someone with a steady job, as well as someone starting up their own company. Understanding that your relationship to those paying you is vitally important, and if overlooked or not seen properly, this relationship can become a problem instead of a solution.

These are your partners. You are the one in charge of your goals and your life. Those who pay you, do so with an expectation of return. What you want is for them to be happy with that return. That is all.

I wanted the people in my neighborhood to enjoy the lemonade. When I was finished making it, I was proud of it. And by the time I was done, I cared a great deal about the people who were paying me, and I understood them better.

My grandfather's suggestion of leaving the table and chairs behind, forced me to understand the people who would pay me.

If you want to build wealth you have to understand that relationship. Who is paying you?

Think of them as partners in your journey to provide for yourself and those you love the life you really want. Incidentally, the next summer, after I had forgotten about the lemonade wagon and had moved on to basketball, some of the neighbors came and asked if I would be delivering lemonade again. It had become something more than just waiting behind a table.

Lesson number two.

A week or so after the lemonade stand had turned into a lemonade wagon, my grandfather took me to a national park near our home. We stood at the edge of a river and he told me about the trees and the animals that lived there. But then he asked me a question:

How did this river get here?

He asked me to figure out for myself how the river got there. I told him that it came from that direction, and pointed up river. So he walked me up river a ways, and asked me again. I told him I didn't know. So, he walked me further up river until we hit a small stream pouring down the side of a hill and emptying into the river.

The river comes from this, I said.

He asked me how all the water in the river could fit in one small stream.

I told him that there were many streams. From all over.

He smiled. Happiness, he said, and success in life, should not come from only one tiny little stream, that isn't how things work. If you want to do something the size of the river, if you want to be something the size of the river, you'll need a lot of these little streams.

Whatever our measure of success, whether it be tied to time, money, or happiness, we can learn to add to it and turn it from a stream into a river by following and implementing a few simple changes in our lives.

Notice I said simple. I did not say easy.

The End at the Beginning

Why would you read a book like this? What do you want from your life? If you don't know, it is time to figure it out.

With an ever changing economic climate our ability to provide the lifestyle we want for ourselves and our loved ones has become problematic. Before we talk about how we can change the direction of our life we need to see things more clearly. Let's ask ourselves a few questions:

Who is the boss? Who is in charge?

It is hard to see the forest for the trees as we make our way through life. But it is important for all of us to know who exactly is in charge here. If we make the assumption that we alone control our destiny, then we might be making a mistake and not looking at the facts.

Who pays you?

This might be our first thought. The person who pays me is in charge, right? I work for someone, and they are the boss. What they say goes, right?

Wrong. They may have a certain position with different responsibilities, but this is your life we are talking about here. They are paying you. It is important to think of them as partners or associates, but you are the one providing your own abilities and expertise, and you have the freedom to remain in a relationship with them or move in a different direction.

Taking yourself seriously is the first step to building wealth.

Who do you pay?

When considering the elements around you that control you it is easy to overlook the places and activities we give our money to. In some ways, this relates more to who the boss is. Does your time and money go toward the well-being of yourself and your family? Does it go toward entertainment? Does it disappear?

Understanding your priorities gives you clarity to build wealth.

In this book we will be focusing on who is paying you, but we must always keep in mind why we are planning for the future, why we desire to build wealth.

Where to Start

There are many definitions of 'Maturity,' but the one which relates most to wealth building concerns taking responsibility for your own life.

It isn't your parent's fault, it isn't your school's fault, it isn't your spouse's fault.

It is your responsibility.

Waking up from the childish daze which keeps you behind the card table, sitting in chairs hoping someone will happen along and give you some money, is the first step.

Get up.

Starting to think about your own place in the world around you, and changing the way you view building wealth sets you automatically apart from others.

One reason so many people desire wealth is laziness. Its remarkable how many people miss this when they start evaluating themselves. If laziness is the factor driving your desire to build wealth, you might as well stop reading.

Laziness doesn't build wealth.

Why do you think the lottery is so popular?

Getting rich quick will always be a scam. It starts you on the path of laziness. It inspires only more laziness.

But building lasting wealth requires something of us. It may be the most wonderful experience of your life, but it will often not be the easiest.

Is it worth it?

Not all of us have rivers handed to us on a silver platter. Often we are given a small stream, an income that can sustain us. And there is nothing wrong with keeping and maintaining our stream. This is in fact where we all must begin.

But if we want something more. If our heart yearns to ride the rapids of real change then we must learn to make our stream become a river.

It is the kind of work, few people are up for. It can be difficult work. In terms of turning our stream into a river, we have to find the tools to attract more and more water. This may not be money; our success might be measured in more subtle ways. We may desire to attract more and more talent to our business, more and more inspiration to our artistic endeavors.

The principle is the same. To build real long lasting wealth and success our stream has got to become a river.

Setting our sights

Alright, so where do we begin?
The first step is honest self-evaluation. When building a canal, we don't see first a man with a shovel, randomly begin anywhere he feels, there are sometimes years of preparation.

Now, luckily for us, our success is already a part of who we are and where we are, it will not take years to evaluate, but we must be intentional.

What do you want?

You may quickly answer this question without much hesitation; money, happiness, etc., but it is worth thinking deeply about.

When we think of the things we want from our lives we begin to get a sense of our river.

An engineer would need to know where the river was heading, what its purpose was, before planning anything.

And so with our river.

What do you want? This will determine how all the pieces fall together.

Understanding what you want from your life and what you want to say with your life will help to define just how to set about turning your stream into a river.

So, before we go about turning our stream into a river let us think of concrete answers to a few important questions.

What makes me happy?

What do I want my legacy to be?

How do I honestly measure success?

What makes me come alive?

What are my fears?

What is my work ethic?

Before continuing it would be a good idea to write down specific answers to these questions. Your answers will provide fuel and stamina as you proceed.

Who is paying you?

For my grandfather, this was the first question. The truth was, at the age of eleven, my friend and I simply assumed that someone eventually would.

But no one will. Your stream always starts with you. Whether you've been handed a company from a parent, hired by a friend, or started from the ground up, you are in charge of your stream.

And this is where it all begins.

There are always stories of the person who quite their job, told off the boss, started their own company, and now makes millions selling refurbished socks, but I've never met that person.

If you can't handle your stream, how can you handle a river.

Practicing care with your stream, will create in you and those around you, the confidence to move beyond.

And this is key. Many famous stock market gurus will say that if a company is worth buying than it's worth buying. The price is only one factor. The trend is only one factor.

We sell ourselves short when we dream of someday having a rushing river, when we cannot even deal with our small stream.

This is practice. This is where you can get good at the important things. If you get good at caring for your stream, the river will not carry you away when it comes.

Right now you have the opportunity to practice the skills that will make you proficient in turning your stream into a river.

Right now.
So, who is paying you now? Are you self-employed or have a full time job? Are you a stay at home parent?

This is your stream. The time and resources you have are cultivating your stream right now, and these same skills, can change your life.

Understand that those who pay you are not in charge. If you get yourself out from under that mentality you can engage with them in more positive and effective ways.

Understand that your employer, the person who pays you, is partnered with you in an endeavor which is advantageous to you both.

The same goes for the self-employed. Understanding who pays you and how you sit in relation to them, will offer you the opportunity to meet their needs and desires in a way that was not possible before.

It is not a competition, it is a cooperation.

Many employees come to see their job as a burden. But they do so without a clear picture of who is paying them.

You have something, your time and efforts, and you can get paid for these things. This is what we are calling your stream. This is your success.

Now let me ask you a question: Do you want your stream to become a river?

If you do, then what is more profitable, viewing those that pay you as a burden or as partners in building your stream into a river?

Change is good.

When we start to see them as partners we can begin adding to our stream; adding other partners.

Taking that first step

Now that we've adjusted our thinking, let's look at what it means to go beyond our own stream and begin searching for the next stream.

Before you take that first step it is important to evaluate the kind of river you eventually want. And what kind of next step you desire to make.

Consider a carpenter who wishes to turn his stream into a river. He thinks about starting his own business on the weekends. And this may seem like a good step.

But what if his river did not include working on the weekends. It might be that this stream is only temporary, an important aspect when starting out, but what if there was another way.

What if, when looking first at what he desired from his river, and second his own abilities and interests, he saw his baseball card collection and his love of old baseball memorabilia as an option.

I've met many people who have turned a small love or passion into something great. When it is something you already know, it's all the more easy to turn it into something useful.

Going beyond your stream

It may seem obvious, but after you've begun to understand yourself and your goals better, it is time to step out of your stream. Searching beyond your stream is extremely important.

You could take these next steps, and implement them in your own stream. You may be tempted to find associates or mentors right in your own stream, but it is vital to first go beyond the boundaries of your stream. Take a walk.

Practicing good habits within your stream, will start you on the right path, but to turn your stream into a river, you must go beyond it.

Why?

Because you want your stream to be a river. You want to add. And to add to your stream, you have to go beyond it.

Is it scary?

Of course it is. Anything worth doing will have its difficulties. Not only that, but those first few attempts to go beyond your stream, may cause a strong reaction from those close to you.

This fear and these reactions keep most of us from changing anything in our lives. Those who surround us, as well meaning as they are, can easily put the brakes on our positive change. They can keep us in our stream.

It will be uncomfortable.

This first step can be the hardest for some of us. We like our stream. It's fine enough. But go back to our self-evaluation. What do you want?

If you want a river, you have to get out of your stream.

Partners

I saw a friend of mine begin a business in the food industry and it very quickly began to grow. He was adding partners here and there, and I watched as his stream, began to overflow.

He did not yet have a river.

His stream turned into a swamp. A stagnant pool of standing water. And this was because he chose the wrong partners.

They had become problems themselves rather than helping solve problems.

There is more than one kind of partner; to grow your stream we will focus on three very important categories of partners.

The first of course, are those that pay you. Understanding them as partners in your wealth building is crucial. But our next partner is also crucial.

Mentors

We've all heard it before: Give a man a fish and he'll eat for a day, teach a man to fish, and he'll eat for a lifetime, right? Well, what do we want when we are the man? Do we want a fish? Or, do we want to learn how to fish?

The biggest issue with the mentor relationship is often where to find one. And more importantly, where to find a good one.

This step in wealth building can be difficult. I personally found mentors by accident, on vacation, at my local church.

But what I learned from them was invaluable. They had walked through the process already. They had turned their streams into rivers. They would have the tools and the know-how which, until then, I did not possess.

Associates

These types of partners can be our biggest help and sometimes our biggest hindrance. Associates are those partners we get for specific reasons. These types of partners give us their time in pursuit of a shared goal.

Business partners, tech assistance, brokers, lawyers, employees, employers, baby sitters, the list goes on and on. Because this list depends upon what you are doing when you get out of your stream.

Just as with mentors it is important to think outside our stream. When starting a new business venture, we may think of our friends to join us, but this is often a bad idea. It is the easy way out.

Not what's easy. What's best.

If our goals are clear, and we have arrived outside our stream and have begun the search for new ground to break, new water to find, then we have the freedom and the responsibility to find the best associates possible.

We must think as a manager of a company, not as a person with friends. We all have friends. They may be great friends, but that doesn't mean they would be good associates.

Saving money

We all know about saving money, we've heard about it all our lives. So, why don't we do it. Why don't we save?

The truth is that we have stacked the deck against ourselves. We have put all the odds against our saving. What we put in front of ourselves all day is advertisements, and what we put inside our heads all day is thoughts of getting rid of our money.

On top of this, many of us, due to guilt about saving or some childhood event, will experience a kind of thrill when we spend our money. A thrill which calls to us subtly from behind every purchase.

And so, we have stacked the deck perfectly against our intentions to save, and then we sit about and wonder why we haven't.

Add to this the fact that we often get into a rhythm with our money. Our pay comes in, and the money goes out, then we wait, the pay comes in, the money goes out.

So, what are we to do?

The first step to building wealth is to turn this process around. We have to see the system differently and make it work for us. We have to guide our money into the avenues we want.

If you are not full of self-restraint and control than it is important that you set up a way that is full proof. Some people deal with their money like it is a business, and themselves as the CEO. This can help us see it all more mechanically and with less emotional attachment.

Also, concerning the institutions that your money comes in contact with, you can often set up barriers and rules to guide your money into the proper places. You can take money from your paychecks and have it deposited by your bank into a savings account before you ever see it. Most employers offer similar plans.

There are multiple other tactics to start saving, to start being in control, but the important thing is to get a move on!

Your money will not save itself.

So, sit down with yourself and anyone else it concerns and come up with a plan.

This is an integral part of learning how to deal with your stream, before it becomes a river.

First, make this plan possible. We can all make up plans in a flurry of resolutions and convictions, but making that plan an achievable one is very important.

Second, is to write down your plan. This may sound obvious, but it is invaluable to the process. Once it is written down it becomes a kind of contract.

Third, is to chart out the small goals you need to achieve for your plan to work. This may be changing spending habits, creating an envelope system like my grandmother, or opening another bank account for special savings such as Christmas funds, etc.

Fourth, you must be committed. This means putting yourself in a place where it is impossible to not save. Treating your future as your job. You are not working for the moment, you are working for your future.

Investment as a Way of Life

The stock market can be a terrifying thing for most people. We would rather give our money to an expert and have them decide, but the truth is that now we each have access to all the tools we need.

It is not easy. But again, building wealth is not easy. Learning from those who have come before us is wise, but the world is changing every day. The advice my grandfather received as a young investor won't always work in our day.

It is important to understand your investing goals, and just like starting a business, or any other venture which involves risk, constructing a plan that works is only the first step.

First, it is important to learn all you can about what you want to invest in. If an investment is valuable to you, then it is valuable, and if it is not, no amount of emotional attachment or guilty feeling will change that.

Second, understand the type of risk you are willing to undertake, this will dictate your course.

Third, it is important to practice. This may seem an odd thing to do, but if your interest is in the stock market than it is important to practice trading on paper. This practicing can happen in other areas of investment as well, but you have to be creative and keep learning.

Fourth, like all other things commitment is key. Being a scared investor is never good; being wise is wonderful, cautious, yes, but scared, no. Make your decisions carefully and then act.

To Simplify

The math is always the same, no matter which way you look at it, and if you spend more than you make then your financial goals will always be out of reach.

It helps to see the job of reining in your expenses as 'simplifying.' And simplifying can be fun and easy.

When you amass the information about your weekly, monthly, or yearly expenses you begin to see a picture or a pattern about what is important to you. This picture can help you decide how to manage your money.

We might have a tendency to think about the unnecessary items first, and see these as the things we need to get rid of, but it is important to see the picture honestly. What kind of life do you want? Is it one where you are worried about money all the time and never do anything you want?

Of course not! That is exactly what you are trying to avoid.

But if you simplify your life in such a way that you have lowered many of your expenses, even by a small amount, then saving becomes easier, and also doing those things you love becomes guilt free.

Wouldn't that be wonderful?

You spend only what you make with room in the budget to save for the future, and all this without giving up the things that you love.

But this takes work. It takes effort to find out where your money goes. Most of us don't even want to look into it, we might be ashamed. But the truth is that we have to look into it!

We have to get serious!

This is the difference between those who are free from struggling with their finances and those who keep feeling overwhelmed. It is difficult to bring your finances under control but it is vital.

Simplification can mean many things. It can mean what types of food you buy, to organizing your day or your office.

Making things simple can be complex.

But once you've gone through the hard part, and you have simplified an area of your life, then it becomes simple maintenance. After you clean your office, it is easier to keep it clean.

And again we find ourselves at the moment of commitment. Am I committed to living a simplified life? Even if this means changing certain habits and behaviors I am used to?

If you want to build wealth, this can be one of the most important steps. Commit to simplify!

First, decide what area or areas in your life need simplified. Is it the budget, the weekly schedule, your morning routine, your home office?

Second, write out your plan to simplify. Decide how best to simplify and chart your course.

Third, seek help about simplifying areas you are unsure about. Financially it may be a difficult task, and you may need to seek specific guidance about your specific situation.

Fourth, commit. If you have to, write out a contract and sign it.

What should the streams look like?

When you step beyond your own stream and begin digging another, what do you look for? How do you know what will work?

The answer is you don't know what will work, this is part of the work itself. Many entrepreneurs fail at many of their first attempts.

There are two areas that we can work on when trying to build wealth, we can keep the money we have, and we can get more money. This may sound crude, but it is really this simple.

So once we've understood our own stream better, we've simplified, and we are holding on to more of our money, now what?

How do we choose where to put the shovel?

This is an entirely personal step. This step is one of your own tastes and your own habits and your own desires. What do you want to do?

Taking small jobs to fill in some of our income gaps is really wise. This can lead to more opportunity in the future. Many of us are afraid of this type of 'stream adding', but usually a small job is not permanent. Think of this type of work as a stepping stone, along your journey.

Solving a problem…

Another great way of thinking outside your stream is to look around you for problems you come into contact every day. This is an opportunity!

Instead of working on your flying car idea, while complaining about the horrible finance program you have on your computer, see the finance program as a problem to be fixed and fix it.

This is where some of the best opportunities are.

Also, look into your own life at the things you are passionate about. What makes you come alive? What hobbies do you have that might be turned into a stream? Do you make things? Are you an expert in anything?

We all think of money as a key to success, but what if your river was built of free time? What if that was how you measured your success? Each stream you built would then do its part to give you time for your loved ones and your passions.

What if success for you was the ability to help others? Charity work is essential to many of us, and giving back to others can be the most joyful experience in life. If your success is measured in this, then your streams should be measured by how they afford you more and more opportunity to give back.

Take all of these things as possible streams and then the choice is yours.

Once you've made the decision, start digging. It is that simple! It is in your hands!

Waiting

Becoming a person who knows how and when to wait can be a positive step in turning your stream into a river.

The lazy wait on the front end, the wealthy wait on the back.

You can wait for wealth to fall into your lap, you can complain about money all day, you can even play the lottery, but wealth is not built by the lazy and the waiting.

Streams are turned into rivers through hard work. But sometimes, along the way, it is important to know when to wait.

It is an integral part of maneuvering into success.

There was a man, let's call him Thad, and he was sitting at home waiting for someone to make him wealthy. He hoped that his parents would give him money, he wished his boss would promote him, and he figured his future wife would be wealthy.

Thad's next door neighbor was Janet. Janet was in the same place as Thad, except she wasn't waiting for wealth to just happen. She was digging another stream in her back yard, by growing herbs and selling them at the local farmers market.

She also learned to simplify her life, and while Thad was buying the newest video game, she was learning to paint.

After a few years, Thad was very good at his video game, and Janet had two new streams of income. She had sold some of her paintings online and she was doing well at the farmers market.

After a few more years, Janet started a new stream, it was risky, but she invested in a computer store in a nearby city. Thad decided he would no longer wait around for wealth but would take initiative and started looking for a wealthy woman to marry.

Here is where the waiting switched. Janet had to learn to be patient, she was learning how to wait with wisdom, while Thad had turned himself into a go getter, but it was in the wrong direction.

Getting rich quick schemes don't work because you continue to be the same lazy person you were. You haven't addressed the real issue.

Janet's computer store would do very poorly for the first four years, and she had a choice, she could consider it a failure and move on, or she could stick out the troubled times, knowing the company was solid and should soon start making money, or she could leave.

Sometimes waiting is a bad choice. But sometimes it is the right choice.

Commitment

The road ahead is bumpy. It is a lot of hard work. Turning your stream into a river will mean a lot of serious rearranging. It will not be easy.

Commitment is what is needed, this is not for the faint of heart. Few people will learn and grow, and only a few will learn how to stand up after falling.

The decision to become wealthy and to turn your stream into a river is one that takes courage and determination. You do have what it takes, but will you use what you have?

My grandfather taught me two valuable lessons: know who is paying you, and a river is made from many small streams. This has guided me to happiness and success, and I am forever greatful.

Know where your streams come from. Learn to be efficient and simplify. And commit.

Commit to a change of attitude, commit to new habits, and commit to your future.

The Beginning at the End

Why would you read a book like this? What do you want from your life? If you don't know, it is time to figure it out.

www.ingramcontent.com/pod-product-compliance
Lightning Source LLC
Chambersburg PA
CBHW070341190526
45169CB00005B/1992